Spirit and Flesh Dancing Together as One

By: Sarafia Jones- Hall

Sponsored By: Be it Unto Me INTL Ministries:
Experience The Power Of The Cross
Publisher: 2 Covenant Mogul publishing House
Cover Artist: 2 Covenant Mogul Publishing House
Editor: Ellen McKnight

Copyright © 2016 by **Sarafia Jones-Hall First** Printing. Printed and bound in the United States of America. All rights reserved. No portion of this book may be reproduced in any form or by any means, including information storage and retrieval systems, without written permission from the publisher, except by a reviewer, who may quote brief passages in a review.
Published by Sarafia Jones-Hall.
Website:www.sarafiahall.com
ISBN:978-1535460989

Unless otherwise indicated, all Scripture quotations are from the King James version of the Bible. Scriptures quotations marked (NIV) are taken from the *HOLY BIBLE, NEW INTERNATIONAL VERSION* ® Copyright © 1973, 1978, 1984 by International Bible Society. Used by permission of Zondervan Publishing House. All rights reserved.

The "NIV" and "New International Version" trademarks are registered in the United States and Trademarks office by International Bible Society. Use of either trademarks requires the permission International Bible Society. Scripture quotations marked (AMP) are taken from *The Amplified Bible, Old Testament,* Copyright © 1965, 1987 by the Zondervan Publishing House. *The Amplified New Testament,* Copyright © 1954, 1958,1987 by The Lockman Foundation. Used by permission.

Note: In some Scripture quotations, italics have been added by the author for emphasis only.

Dedication

This book is dedicated to my grandmother Mary Jones, Big momma I miss you and love you so much, you are home with the Lord. Big momma you introduced me to Jesus, if I didn't know him, I wouldn't be walking in my calling now. I would have not gotten to publish this book. Thank you, granny, for your hard wood floors, when I was a little girl that was my first dance studio where I danced my first dance.

I love you!

Acknowledgments

I want to thank my Daddy God for saving & calling me, pulling me out of the rough side of the mountain. I thank you Lord Father for giving me the gift to worship through dance, as well as impart and teach others. I'm thankful to birth out this book that you gave me, I love You Daddy God!

To Terri Vaughn, my sister, my friend and prayer warrior; Terri you never gave up on my dreams even when I wanted to throw in the towel. Thank you for a listening ear and encouraging me to write and open my dance school. Thank you

To Apostle Neddie Moore words cannot express how grateful to God I am for teaching me the spiritual side of God, while revealing revelation of the word and having such a love and liberty of God spirit in your ministry, your love pushed, and the encouragement to go back to school for dance. Thank you.

To Stefanie Hayes my sis, friend, straight up tell me the truth sister, thank you for encouraging me, fasting and praying for me and reading the chapters as I wrote giving me input. You have been with me many years pushing me forward. Thank you.

To My Leaders Bishop Lamont & Lady Taiger Hillard, thank you for being Leaders of integrity. Leaders after God Spirit and excellence thank you for the life changing sermons and the encouraging words. Thank you.

To Apostle Lisa St. Clair, thank you for mentoring and much prayer, much, much, much prayer and standing in the gap for me when I wanted to give up. Thank you.

To (Apostle) Dr. Sandy Murphy, I thank God for you, a woman of integrity and one who believes in pushing those in the kingdom; I thank you for the many connections and pushing me in this season. I've only known you a short time but it seems like years, I have accelerated tremendously. Author to Author may your books become Top Sellers. Thank you for introducing me to an awesome Book Publisher.

To my son and daughter in-law, God sent you right on time, thank you for helping me with videos and photo shoots. I thank you for listening and reading chapters and critiquing, and sharing ideas with me I didn't even know I love you. Thank you.

To my publisher Dr. Serena Washington, there can't be a great book without a great publisher. We met and I knew you were the one to push my project. Thank you for putting the roller blades to my book and helping me to enlarge. I thank you for your excellence and praying with me and encouraging me as we worked to get this project out.

Finally, to My Husband Samuel, thank you for encouraging me to not only write my book; but to finish it. Thank you for taking us out to eat so I didn't have to cook, but you said finish your book. that. Thank you, honey, for your prayers; I love you Sam.

I thank all my friends and co-laborers in the ministry and worship dancers, mentees and spiritual daughters, supporters. **Thank you!**

Author Bio website bio

"Call to Duty" Isaiah 61:1

Evangelist Sarafia Jones-Hall is a native of Waco TX. and has been commissioned to the great city of Houston TX. As an Evangelist, she has been charged to preach the word in season and out of season through any situation. Evangelist Hall operates under a strong prophetic anointing in dance, prayer, intercession; as well as the preached word. Her calling and passion are to impart deliverance, healing, and true worship to the lost and unlearned through mentorship, teaching, and activation of the ministry gifts.

Evangelist Hall has been ministering in the Prophetic Dance Ministry for over fourteen years. She attended Sons of Zadok in 2011 under the teaching of Pastor Sabrina McKenzie- Dancing Preachers International, where she received a Liturgical Certification in dance. Evangelist Hall is the founder and CEO of Dance N2 Ur Deliverance Ministry, which now includes the prophetic School of Dance. Evangelist Hall's commitment is to teach dance, as well as its history from the natural and spiritual side. Her passions are to empower and impart into the youth and set up and build dance ministries while introducing diversity and other cultures to different styles of worship.

Through much adversity, abuse, rejection, and being left for dead, Evangelist Hall dropped out of junior high school feeling great desperation. Despite her situation she was given a way of escape, as she loved to dance. Music brought light into her life and started the transformation from hopelessness to faith. God gave her a way of escape, and she wants to pour that same spirit of perseverance and endurance in many. Evangelist Hall knows there is a level of compassion, patience and understanding we must have, to connect with our youth and those that are broken. She believes in giving back to the community and can boldly take ministry back home to the streets and outside the four walls of the church. Also, her greatest passion is for the broken, wounded, and the castaways. God gave her a way of escape, and she wants to pour that same spirit of perseverance and endurance into many.

Evangelist Hall is a certified Zumba instructor and preparing to be a certified personal trainer. She is currently instructing kids in fitness and dance. Evangelist Hall has several more books she plans to birth out in "2017-2018" Her 2nd book will be released June "2017" Titled: *My Chapter 2016 Journey*. She is married to Prophet Samuel Hall, and they currently reside in Houston, TX. with their family. *Contact her on Facebook or website:www.sarafiahall.com*

Contents

Chapter 1
Spirit and Flesh at War
Chapter 2
Conditioning the flesh and not the spirit
Chapter 3
Conditioning of our Spirit
Chapter 4
One body, many members' (connectivity)
Chapter 5
Divided we fall
Chapter 6
Mission Aborted To Much Flesh
Chapter 7
In Position No Submission
Chapter 8
Jezzie taking the platform
Chapter 9
He wants it All
Chapter 10
Dance Away of Escape
Chapter 11
Consecration and consummation
Chapter 12
Cover Yourself
Chapter 13
Biblical colors with meaning and scripture

Spirit and Flesh Dancing Together as One

Greek/ Hebrew praise dance words

Bibliography?
Dance…. away of escape

As a little girl I had to boogie-woogie, I just loved music and with music there was the love and joy of the dance. I believe when happy feet came out they got the concept from me. As a toddler, I was always moving dancing, bouncing, shaking my little hips (well imaginary hips), shaking my little diaper (smile).

My family loved music, I remember, my mom had this old antique stereo and she would always put it on K104 FM as we cleaned our home or had family bar-b-ques. Music and dance have been a big part of our family, a dance contest is what it was about. As I got older my grandmother bought me a musical box and when we would wind it up and open the lid the ballerina would turn around and around; I was so amazed of how she twirled. I would imitate her; I just knew I was a ballerina too (smile).

The posture and form came easy to me, no one had taught me or even told me about ballet, but I knew deep down inside that one day I would dance like the ballerina in the jewelry box. On rainy days, I would put on my socks and get on the tips of my toes and twirl and spin fast, then slow, spin up high and spin down low until I became dizzy and plopped down and hit the floor. Oh! How I loved my Granny's shiny wood floors. I would run, slide, spin, and dance. I had never been to a dance studio but I imagined that they had floors like my granny's floors.

If I could remember, music and dance influenced me at any time. I would disappear to another place, another time, a place of peace, of joy or just have dancing fever; every time I heard music or a beat, I had to bust a move; this was day after day and year after year. When I reached adulthood, I would get invited to the dance clubs and bars, but I soon realize the club life was not my thing. One day a light switch came on and I realized I could dance, dance, dance. At age 23 I began to go to the clubs and I would dance the whole night. I was confused as to why so many people were sitting or standing against the walls. I would dance so much I sweated off all my makeup. I did that club thing a few times; but I wasn't satisfied…there was something missing on the inside.

Early one morning after leaving the club, I felt a different conviction fall on me (I thought.... look at you out all night dancing with the devil, and those moves you were making are not pleasing to God. I would have been put out of the church and Holy oil poured on me). Yes, I was saved and in the club shaking what my momma gave me. Well little did I know God had called me his worshipper? I began to see the Lord more and the club life began to fade quickly, but not completely. As I begin to seek God about the feelings I felt when I would hear praise and worship music, and the sound of the drums, my spirit would awake and my body would respond with movements, radical movements. Tears would run down my face and at times, and no one else was moving, but I couldn't keep my hands down and stop my feet from moving. Ahhh! It was worship, I had found it and I fell in love with it because it was the place I was one with my Lord. Our intimate place! In this place, I didn't care who was watching, I was dancing with my father.

Even though this was a breathtaking feeling, I still found myself clubbing again and going to church and singing in the choir. I even had the boldness to drink wine coolers, their effect on me led to a one-night stand. I felt horrible and so ashamed when I woke up the next day. When I went to church that morning, I cried out to God; it seemed

like every song we sang and the sermon that was preached just stuck a dagger to my flesh making me feel guiltier. Today I'm grateful because that was a spirit of conviction.

When we fall and are truly sorrowful we should all experience a heart of conviction. Drum roll please!! The day came that I was introduced to praise dancing, I was 26 years old and was so overwhelmed with joy, little did I know I was about to find out why I was so drawn to music and movement. (I was discovering my purpose).

God is so awesome! I remember experiencing my first praise dance and asked to join the dance ministry. When I got introduced to praise dance, I had been through a lot of heart ache, pain and disappointment, not to mention two divorces; yes, at age 26. When praise dance was first introduced to me it was not at the church that I belonged to. We were attending a full fledge Baptist church. At the time, they didn't believe in praise dance or women preachers.

The Lord allowed me to go to another church for a very short season, and I was taught praise dance, although the enemy was fighting me with fear, low self-esteem and insecurity. But I so enjoyed and loved it such a freedom and relief from everything. Things were beautiful in my world, I was at a church where I was not judged and I could be used through dance. I was excepted!

As we all know some good things must come to an end, especially when there are some unresolved issues. The reason I had left the Baptist church and went to this new church was because of church hurt, but the Lord said I had to go back to my home church because of how and why I had left. I returned back to my home church; I believe God honored my speedy return and obedience because soon afterwards we started our dance ministry.

The Lord opened doors. I was able to teach, help the women and teens in dance. My heart was really for the little children, we began the children's dance ministry; it was called "Wings." I really loved teaching the children, although all of this was very new to me and I had no previous training or teaching experience, but I found out the Holy Spirit will teach you how to teach especially when He has called and anointed you to do it. Not only did he teach me how to do the movements, but he taught me how to teach through the Holy Spirit the word of God. As a praise dancer, we are literally preaching with our bodies.

I felt like the time was right and wrong, being such a wounded and insecure woman, not knowing where I fit in. But God knew and had a plan and purpose for me I that I wasn't aware of. Because of past hurts of being frowned up on, always talked about, I had many insecurities. Many times, I felt inadequate and dumb; these feelings were crippling me in a lot of areas of my life. Before I found myself, I looked to others for my approval. But I'm grateful that as years went by, God sent season women to teach mentor and minister to me. Years down the road, I began to receive deliverance in several areas and started growing. I continued to learn as I was relating to other women that overcame similar struggles and disappointments. Through there testimonies and support I began to be pushed into my purpose and my destiny, more than ever in the first year of my dance ministry.

I thought I was delivered in a lot of areas, the enemy wanted to keep me bound with the spirit of fear. I was very afraid to look at the faces of the people in the audience because of what the enemy was saying they were thinking of me as they watched me minister. Therefore, I would dance with my eyes closed. I was literally terrified to look at the people because I could see spirits on them; while still not knowing my gift and the calling on my life. I didn't want to stop dancing so my solution was dance with my eyes closed, sadly to say. I did that for about a year, and then I would find someone I knew and felt comfortable to look at.

After a few years I was able to look at the people; this came through much healing and deliverance. One beautiful Saturday the Lord began to speak to me; He whispered my dance name; He said broken vessel of praise. I was in awe that God named me. And what The Lord said was in my brokenness I would come back and give Him Praise! Glory Hallelujah!

The Lord opened a door for me through dance ministry and I realized I had a religious mindset and only a little word in me even though being in church from a little girl up to age 26 that's all I knew. But at age 28, I learned the Spirit of God the worshiper of God the realm and dimensions of God, the prophetic of God, the apostolic anointing of God. Ruler of the Spirit of God I learned the love of God, I learned in him I was able to be transformed by the renewing of my mind and I was able to embrace the calling on my life as a prophetic dancer, warrior Dancer As well as embrace the dance ministry God had given me
"Dance n2 Ur Deliverance" After nine years as broken vessels of praise, the Lord changed my name to "Dancer of Eradication. After he Named me a year later the Holy Spirit asked me did I know what that meant. I answered no. I was unction in my spirit to define "eradication"

Merriam Webster Define as: *1. To pull up roots destroy completely; put an end to. synonyms: eliminate, get rid of, remove, obliterate; exterminate, destroy, annihilate, kill, wipe out; abolish, stamp out, extinguish, quash; erase, efface, excise, expunge, expel; nuke, wave goodbye to* again Dance away of escape.

Prologue

What is liturgical Dance? (Why Do I Do It?)

Liturgical dance is worship using the entire body; all our limbs are used for edification, and reverence of the Lord; while experiencing connectivity of oneness with the Holy Spirit. Liturgical dance is freedom in our mind, body and spirit. While using different genres of dance to interpret a song or the word. Liturgical dance is not natural but super natural.

Liturgical dance is dancing with the King, as we dance before the King, we are preparing the way for the lost to see the King. Liturgical dance can be very prophetic and you can experience great revelation and deliverance through the dance. It is a gift and a call to minister in the dance.

Why do I dance? I love worship in the dance, it's my passion, my desire, my next heartbeat. I dance because God spoke to me and told me to switch partners; that he would use the worshiper in me to change lives of my love ones and those that are bound.

The dance is my place to be sustained and it gives me a way of escape from trials and tribulations of this world. I dance because God chose me to dance. I experienced the joy and liberty of dance as a little girl. I couldn't sit still if music or a beat came into my presence, I had to dance. I dance realizing that there is power in the dance; dance speaks life to dead things.

We as worshipers must snatch people right up out of the pit of hell, it worked for me. I believe that liturgical dance consumes the atmosphere for healing and deliverance while capturing the souls of the lost and broken hearted. I witnessed these miraculous things right before my eyes. I dance to let satan know that he is bound and will stay bound; Jesus has set us free and we will stay free. As a dancer (worshiper) I know that I am equipped and being more equipped to go into the realm of the spirit to devour satan's plans and tactics against the body of Christ. I dance because I love the experience of my Lord embracing me while I dance him with me and me with Him. Spirit and flesh Dancing Together as One.

Matthew 26:41

Watch and pray, that ye enter not into temptation: the spirit indeed is willing, but the flesh is weak.

Spirit and flesh dancing together as one

Chapter 1

Spirit and flesh at war Matthew 26:41

Our spirit and flesh are always at war because the flesh wants to do things its way. We were born in sin and shaped in iniquity, so from the beginning of time there has been a war with our flesh. Our flesh is weak and desires its own way. The spirit is willing and possesses liberty, loyalty and a selfless will. The flesh is greedy, selfish, puffed up an arrogant. The only way these two can walk together, one must bow down and submit to the other. And even in our giving up our will to the Spirit of the living God there is still a war going on.

Therefore, we know our flesh is sinful and prideful, but the Spirit of God is loving, humble and pure without blemish or spots. The flesh must submit to the Spirit of God, His will, His ways and His thoughts. When the flesh submits that means the flesh has given up self-will. Now how does this happen you may ask.

There must be a daily crucifixion of the flesh to walk and operate in the Spirit of God. We have to have a fasted and disciplined lifestyle know this because it doesn't happen overnight and requires a true commitment. Dancers, sin will easily weigh you down, lay it aside, and be free of it. Walk in the liberty that Jesus paid the price for. From the get go, we must know it is not about us, but all about Him that He may be glorified in and through our worship.

Dancers we should have a repentant heart keeping our slate clean before God, repenting with a sincere and pure heart. That will keep us in good standing with God and it keep us humble. Worshipers we must get to a place where we surrender all to the will of God; that includes our desires, thoughts and our gifts, as well as talents. We should surrender our voice to the voice of God, our ears to His mouth, total surrender of our body so that He can use us and get the Glory.

Dancers, this is not an easy task ask Paul, he wrote "when I go to do right, evil is always present". But God said in his word that He would give us a way of escape through prayer, fasting and eating the word of God. We know the spirit is willing but the flesh is weak. We should continue to ask the Holy Spirit to abide in us and us in Him. As spirit and flesh beings, the flesh is always at war with the spirit. As worship dancers, we want to kill our flesh. Our worship has to be pure and not tainted with transgression. We must always consecrate ourselves before we dance before the Lord so we can stand strong against the devil's tactics of lust, perversion, pride, ego, jealousy, offense, arrogance and so forth. Also, we should carefully choose the music we listen to.

All songs that are played over the air waves, music that we listen to has a message. Indeed, there is a message in the music. Discerning the spirit attached to the music is important. Because someone sings a spiritual song, or a worship leader leads the congregation to worship, does not mean that person has the right spirit or that they are saved. Just as the worldly music have a spirit, worship music has a spirit too. We must guard our ears to keep our temple clean. We don't want to surround ourselves with the wrong music because it can send a confusing message especially to those that we are ministering to.

Say for instance, you were preparing to minister in two weeks at your local church, in your free time you decided to listen to some secular music which is talking about sex drugs and suicide. This type of music is unhealthy to the converted spirit. Believe it or not, you just opened the door to some wicked spirits, possibly allowing them to attach themselves to you. Not only will this affect you while ministering, but when you minister, these sinful spirits are being released into the atmosphere. These evil spirits search for the unsaved souls and attempt to prevent them from receiving the uplifting from the worship and the release during the preached word from the pastor. The Spirit and flesh are at war once again with greater warfare. Let's look at this example, a young lady came to church for deliverance with sex and suicide on her mind; she knows if she can just make it to the house of the Lord, she can get her deliverance. A beautifully dressed worship Dancer comes out and begins to minister in dance and while dancing she touches the young lady with the sex and suicide demons, now that spirit has just gotten ignited. Instead of this person getting delivered and set free, the transformation of those spirits has taken place and those spirits just got stronger now and deliverance has been hindered or aborted.

Now this young lady has to fight even harder to get free. Is she may lose her life because the dressed-up worship dancer who looked good on the outside, but is filthy on the inside. And believe it or not, the lady who came to get her deliverance dies spiritually or physically, you, the minister of dance is now guilty of murder of a spiritual death and her blood is on your hands. I advise you to think twice before ministering before God and his people, because the flesh that listens to the secular music and has no desire to repent or even a thought of repenting has now hindered someone's deliverance. We must kill our flesh daily. Truly there is a war going on in the inside of us we must clean our spirit and stay in constant communion with the Holy Spirit. Pray Lord create in me a clean heart and renew the right spirit in me

Steps to calm the war of our flesh & Spirit

1. Must be saved
2. Prayer life
3. Fasting lifestyle
4. Daily Word
5. Daily Repentance
6. Be honest with God and self
7. Use discernment with music
8. Desire to be more like Christ

1 John 2:16 (NLT)

For the world offers only a craving for physical pleasure, a craving for everything we see, and pride in our achievements and possessions. These are not from the Father, but are from this world.

Chapter 2
Conditioning the flesh and not the spirit...1John 2:16

The worldly way of thinking is condition, condition. Practice makes perfect. You are how you look, who kicks straighter and leaps the highest is the greatest. It's all about you. You must impress everyone, they need to see you. It's all about you. The world is encouraging you to be great no matter the cost. They say get much training, perfect all your moves, exercise, change your eating habits. Get more and more training. You have to look the best and you have to be the best. Everyone is watching. Trainers, diets etc.

Now you know that you're ready to dance anywhere, you're confident (so bring it) dance at the church, dance at the wedding, you're invited to dance for the school talent show or benefit program at the Civic Center. As far as you know, you have done all you need to do to dance before God and His people. Knowing that you got it going on and the people have pumped and primed you, and all eyes are on you; they shout and tell you how good of a dancer you are. Then even suggest you sign up for the "So You Think You Can Dance" competition or maybe even convince you to audition for American Idol. All the things that are feeling good to your flesh.

Now it's Sunday you have picked out the most colorful and most elegant garment so you can show everyone how you practiced and all the dance techniques you have learned. Now it's Lights! Camera! Action! You're on the platform of your church, standing tall, feeling proud because it's your day. Pleased with the garment you have chosen knowing that this is the one that will make your dance look fabulous. Now you think, all the people will love me. You have worked really hard and spent many hours of practice to perfect this dance and the techniques you have learned. It's show time and you are ready for the stage. Wrong!!! You have missed the main ingredient. You are missing JESUS and His Anointing.

Forgetting that this is not a dance recital, but a mission to usher in the presence of God, to saturate the atmosphere with praise and adoration to Him, while allowing healing and deliverance to take place. There are many dance ministries that condition the physical body, but they forget all about the spiritual side by just putting on a show that you orchestrated leaving the Spirit of God out.

I just want to ask you a few questions about some things you witnessed during a Dance being ministered.

1. Did the dancers have technique?
2. Did you feel or sense the spirit of God?
3. Were they covered, upper body, hips and legs?
4. Did you feel like you were being ministered to or performed for?
5. Were the dance moves provocative or spiritual?

We need to ask these questions and observe when we see dancers, dance, ministries, minister. Is it more flesh or operation in God's Spirit?

John 4:23-24

23 Yet a time is coming and has now come when the true worshipers will worship the Father in the Spirit and in truth, for they are the kind of worshipers the Father seeks. 24 God is spirit, and his worshipers must worship in the Spirit and in truth."

Chapter 3

Conditioning of our spirit .... John 4:23-24

How do I condition my spirit to become pliable to the spirit of the living God? We must be in tune with God and sensitive to His presence. As we are in tune with the Holy Spirit we will know that we have been called in or Dance to usher in his presence of God through worship and dance. We will be able to identify our flesh in the flesh of others as we submit, obey and lay before the Lord and allow him to prune us and make us. Then we will become true worshipers as the Lord desires.

Scripture John 4;23–24 but the hour come in now is when the true worshipers shower worships the father in spirit and in truth for the father seek such to worship him god is a spirit in they that worship him must worship him in spirit and in truth.

Conditioning our spirit has nothing to do with the flesh but to be submitted and humble. After we have answered the call then we must get busy. We must study the word of God that speaks about dance and worship in the church. We must study the history and be a student of the word of God study the word Old/ New Testament as well as the very origin of certain movements and different cultures. As we know all dance is not welcome in the church and neither is all attire. This is the beginning of conditioning your spirit so that our flesh will become subject to the Lord to receive clear instructions and be able to deliver the message with power.

As dancers, we are ministers of Christ and there should be a great conviction when we dance the dance of the world and not of the spirit. Worship Dance is an honor and a privilege from God above, it is sacred and Holy. Let's keep it that way. Dancers, the dance you do on the dance floor at the club does not reverence the Lord God, nor is it fit for the church and dance ministry. As we allow God to prune us, shape us and make us we will minister the dances that will bring change and deliverance.

Dance leaders we must teach sound doctrine and cut the flesh and not allow the worship to be contaminated. Cut sin but make sure you are not in the sin. Dance is beautiful and a powerful ministry tool. Dancers take classes, dance workshops, and get educated. Many have come from the world and are not taught holiness, but have a desire to dance for the Lord.

We have to be conditioned by the word and through impartation. Dancers, anytime we get a new position on a job we are trained for that position, the same takes place in the kingdom of God. We go to conferences to learn and become very good at what we do. We as worshipers want to minister in excellence. The word of God is the best spirit conditioner along with wise counsel and impartation. Study dance scriptures, ask questions, and purchase books, just like this one. Be equipped with tools to advance the kingdom of God

Chapter 4

Dance is a way of connectivity

Our mind and body must first connect to receive instructions and then export what has been imported into the body. Look at your body and see how God has shaped and created us. He created us to worship, glorify and praise Him through the dance and song. Our bodies are designed to dance to worship.

Walk with me as I go into the structure of how our amazing God has designed each part of our body, how it uniquely fits together. Our head is on top which includes our eyes, ears, the mouth, nose and most importantly our brain. Each part of our body is perfectly positioned and has important functions as a dancer and worshiper.

Music must first reach our ears which send signals to alert the brain that sends a corporate signal to our whole entire body. Now our body is really charged. Movement begins to automatically take place as we do chorography that activates the nerves. The body is built in a way that even the nerves in the blood flowing throughout the body will flow through one particular part or parts for the other parts of our body to be activated.

Just as the nerves in the blood stream are positioned in a certain way, so is the body case set up a certain way so that all body parts can function in unity. Let's take a look at the position of the head which sits up on the neck up on our shoulders which gives the head a firm and stable foundation, one that doesn't waiver. The shoulders are very important because they support the head and the neck which protects the brain which is the computer or motherboard of the body functions.

The neck helps the head to shift in different positions and angles. The shoulders also support the arms which are joined by ball and socket. The arms are significant for raising up the height of worship and show signs of surrenderance. Look at the upper and lower parts of our body. So far, we have the upper body that's operated by the five natural senses which are smell, touch, sight, taste, sound all motions. We look at the lower part of the body; it's made more for strength, lengthening, height, weight and deepness. The upper and lower body are attuned to one another because the whole body must function together as one entity. In dance, this is in the physical realm, but in the spiritual realm all we need is worship in submitted obedience. The two, flesh and spirit will connect as the one dancing together.

But if the flesh and spirit don't connect, true worship will not take place because we have many members, but the body is disconnected which leads to malfunction in our worship to God. This would stop us from giving Him all the glory, honor and praise which is due Him. Also, it stops the anointing from flowing which hinders deliverance and healing taking place in the atmosphere; that's why we must be connected whole body, mind and soul.

The knee bone has to be connected to the thigh bone and the thigh bone connected to the hip bone for the proper movement to take place in the natural, so it is in the spirit.

Amos 3:3 (ASV)

Can two walk together, except they be agreed?

Chapter 5

Divided we fall .... Amos 3:3 (ASV)

How can two walk together unless they agree? The flesh must submit to the spirit of Almighty God (Holy Spirit) and His instructions. If the physical and the spiritual don't connect with God, He will not be glorified and we would have a tainted worship that would rise and stink before the nostrils of God. We want him (God) to smile and smell the sweet fragrance of our worship. We must feed our spirit man and deny the gratifying of our flesh. As we know a winning team collaborates and works together.

When there is division, there is no crown. So as a worshiper, we must kill the flesh daily, work out our own soul salvation. And just know if we want to experience God and worship like never before we must crucify our flesh, our desires and be unified with Christ like never before. There should be a thirst and hunger for righteousness, we should have such a burning desire to be in the bosom of God knowing that as we long for Him and give our total selves to Him, He will show up.

Believers, worshipers, psalmist, minstrels, servants of the most High God, we must walk in unity with the Holy Spirit. There must be a deliberate walk in holiness, obedience and submission. Let me share with you, there is a danger in doing ministry not consecrated or connected to the Holy Spirit.

If we are not connected that means we are operating in the flesh, that's without the anointing. It is the anointing that destroys the yokes, not our leaps, spins and kicks, no matter how high you kick, jump or leap, yokes will remain. If we are not operating under the Spirit of the living God, the wrong spirits can attach to us; such as jezebel, divinity, pride, sabotage, arrogance etc. Worshipers, we are ministers of the gospel, revealing the word through movement. We are worship leaders (dancers).

Let's take a look at the word "dancer." Webster's definition…. to engage in or perform a dance. If we are not careful and connected to the anointing, we will merely be putting on a performance. This is very dangerous, for the word of God says; in (2 Corinthians 10:4 for the weapons of our warfare are not carnal, but mighty through God to the pulling down of strong holds). We are called and chosen to pull down strongholds, not being carnal and making our flesh feel good, as well as others. That is not our purpose, but our purpose is to get them delivered and push them closer to the presence of God. Carnality is being divided from God and His presence, once carnality sits in then comes the fall. As worship leaders and dancers, we must consecrate ourselves, mind, body and spirit. How can two walk together unless they agree, the flesh and the spirit have to have the same appetite, or dissatisfaction will rise and sickness will take place because the flesh will vomit up the word and the spirit is going to spew out what is not like God, now there is war going on, divided we fall.

Chapter 6

Mission aborted Too much FLESH......

In 2016 the dance ministry, mime, hip-hop etc., is booming, everyone is dancing, everyone wants to dance, teach, direct, is this what it is Right? Wrong! Everyone wants to be in the dance ministry, and many are; but, how many have NOT sought God to see if this is their calling and if they were chosen and equipped for this ministry. What I've notice is with quite a few ministries; the ministry has great technique and can perform very well. I have seen dancers and was very amazed by their technique and dancing ability. Really great performances that touched my heart and dancing ability. But was performance, the right song for the right occasion. But when I looked deeper I saw exactly what I thought I saw, I saw them, all of them and the more the crowd hollered, the more I saw them which equaled to, too much FLESH!!!

You may ask what do I mean? Let's leap together and I'll explain. When a person puts on a performance, first we look at their posture. What is their posture? Is it prideful, is it fleshly, is it lustful, is it humble, is their posture submissive, is their posture ministry driven or, is it all eyes on me posture. Our posture is very important, it speaks and says that we are performing or we are ministering. What is performing or performance? Performing means to present a form of entertainment to an audience.

News flash! We are not performers, but ministers of God through dance and worship. When God opens doors, and place us on a platform, it is all about giving Him all the glory and ushering in the atmosphere to set the captives free while preparing the atmosphere for deliverance and healing and miracles, through the word of God. We are to prepare the way, not get up there and show off what we have learned in school. For example, our ballet techniques or think we've got it going on and trying to show off for family and friends.

You may ask what is a dance minister or is there any such thing as Dance ministers? The answer is yes; a dance minister, ministers the word through motion, movement, expression, most of all with a selfless heart. A dance minister unfolds, unravels the word of God creating a clear picture of God's glory. A dance minister brings the words alive from your hearing right to your eyes that see deep in to your hearts and spirit while unveiling revelation of depth and perception of the word.

Dance ministers minister prophecy, healing and deliverance through movement of the dance especially when there are no words. God will speak if you are called and anointed and breakthroughs will take place, yolks and burdens will be lifted. As we are submitted and totally surrendered to God, change will take place.

What is the down fall of being too fleshly? We miss the mark. We miss the purpose of God choosing us and anointing us. Great hindrance will take place and many will miss their deliverance and salvation. Because it is the anointing that destroys yolks, not our many years of dance classes. If there is too much foolishness, healing and deliverance can't take place and the glory of God can't fall.

Mission aborted too much flesh

Dance ministers or any leader MUST HAVES:

1. must pray and read God's word
2. Must Live a fasting life
3. Must be selfless
4. Must be submissive to the will of God
5. Must die to flesh/ operate in holiness
6. Must walk in humility and not pride

7.   Must be teachable

8.   Must be saved

As you read about the MUST HAVES for a dance minister, place a check next to the ones you are and an X next to the ones that you are not. If you check off all these or the majority, that may mean you need to be trained or retrained and while you are in training sit down and allow God to purge you and make you a great leader.

Job 22:21-22 (NIV)

21 "Submit to God and be at peace with him; in this way prosperity will come to you. 22 Accept instruction from his mouth and lay up his words in your heart.

Chapter 7

In position but no Submission

Position ----- put in a certain place and or over a station, leadership, dance ministry, teacher and or praise and worship leader. First, to be positioned in a place, we must first make sure that it is where God has placed and positioned us at that time. When in a place of leadership, we must portray Christ and His works. Jesus Christ set the greatest example of how to position ourselves. Jesus, the Messiah, King of Kings and Lord of Lords came into the earth positioned low, meek and mild. He positioned His posture with humbleness and humility.

As Jesus walked this earth He continued to position himself low, humble, meek and mild. Jesus who knows all and sees all, who studied and talked the talked and walked the walked as well as trained his followers daily, led by example. Jesus walked in humility and submission to the Father, His father, our Father, God. Jesus kept his posture and position; He only did and said as the Father gave instruction. Heb.3:17 Jesus did many miracles and stood on many great platforms, amongst Kings and Queens, yet He stayed in the position of humbleness. As Jesus positioned himself and walked in humility, the power of God was able to come through him and bring life to the dead, healing to the sick, great deliverance from demonic forces, souls saved and the hungry fed.

You may be wondering why am I doing Bible school about Jesus, because just as Jesus exemplified God and the word we do also in our low/high and important positions. Dancers we can be so arrogant, hateful and prideful as well as rebellious. Because many think they have arrived. One reason is because some have been in dance since they were 2 years old and now they are older and have gained great technical skills through training, received salvation, and the church has a praise dance ministry and now you can show off all you have learned over the years. While failing to realize that training is great, but without Jesus' anointing and a humble spirit you are out of position.

Jesus taught and had no arrogance or pride, so what makes us think we can minister, dance, sing, preach with arrogance and pride. We can't because God will not be glorified and his ailing people will not get healed, delivered and or set free through your dance ministry.

Dancers let me say this just because your leader hasn't had as much training as you don't mean you can take over the position as the leader, or buck your leader. Instead they should submit to their leadership and grab a hold of the vision and see how you can help push and grow the dance ministry. Trying to fast and take over a position that you are not spiritually qualified for can be disastrous to you and the ministry. So, continue to follow the program, be committed to that ministry, be prayerful and prove to God that you are faithful and your time of promotion will come. God knows when you are ready for that promotion. Don't go trying to show yourself up, use self-control and be patient. If you believe God has called you to this particular ministry, then under the direction of your leader you help to bring forth the vision for the church.

We talked about being low, low is the way to go, walking in humility at all times. Worshipers we should always be vessels of honor molded and pruned for the master's use. Not for our own self gain to be seen or heard. God hasn't changed his mind, He wants us to be trained and equipped with all that, but He's still seeking true worshippers, those sold out for Christ and willing to give their gifts and talents back to the Father so they are used for His Glory.

Just in case you still don't quite understand what submission is let's go to the dictionary and the word of God. Here is the meaning of submission…. the condition of being submitted, humble, or compliant, submitting to the authority or control of another.

Let's stop right here and have a Selah moment. Dancers/Worshipers are anointed and appointed for such a time as this. We should be able to submit while respecting and holding up our dance leaders, that one God has placed over the dance ministry, the one God has ordained and appointed for this time and season in your life and your ministry. Your Pastor, leaders, mentor, trust their leadership and the position they have in your life.

Worshipers our job is to hear from God and bring forth the vision that our leaders have shared with us from the Lord, while working together as many member/worshipers but one body, one movement (1 cor.12:14-18. We must have the same motives and desires that execute and breakup the hardened hearts and wounded souls and bring them to the place of peace and freedom through our dance of unity, oneness and love, one move, breath and sound.

Watch the Power of God change the atmosphere, we will experience the presence of His Shekinah Glory fall...as pure worship saturates the atmosphere. Remember great leaders follow and undergird their leaders and through submission, serving, laboring in love, supporting and operating in obedience, in our due season God will remember and elevate us. Again, I say worshipers stay low. Let God do the Raising!

1 King 21-14-15

14 Then they sent to Jezebel, saying, Naboth is stoned, and is dead. 15 And it came to pass, when Jezebel heard that Naboth was stoned, and was dead, that Jezebel said to Ahab, Arise, take possession of the vineyard of Naboth the Jezreelite, which he refused to give thee for money: for Naboth is not alive, but dead.

Chapter 8

Jezzie has taken the Platform ...1 King 21-14-15

You may be wondering, who is Jezzie? Let's look to see if you know him or her or if she or he is "YOU" ... Jezzie can come in many forms and fashion. She can portray to be one way, but her motives don't line up with the word.

(Scenario)... Jazzier just joined your church and she is a worship dancer, mime, singer, etc. She approaches the dance leader about joining your dance ministry. She seems to be very gifted and anointed and has several years of dancing in ministry. She asked to join your dance ministry and you say yes. Now let's see if she is who she says she is.

Jezzie has been a part of your dance ministry about a week she has suggestions on how she thinks you should teach the new dance. Suggestions are good and harmless, so you think. Second week you notice her ignoring you and doing her own moves and suggesting to the rest of the team, doesn't this work better. Some of the team members are agreeing with her even to the point to say, wow! I can tell you have taken dance classes, you move so beautifully. As the weeks go by some of the dancers are not responding to you the dance leader as they normally would. Ok, it's been four weeks and it is the Sunday your dance team will minister and it appears the connection amongst the team is off; the ladies are being short with you and one another. Jezzie has come in very late with an attitude and spirit of confusion. You say to everyone let's prepare to pray, Jezzie says why pray now we are about to go up next and I have to go over my moves, we all need to practice., Jezzie asks the other dancers if they want to practice, some of them agree, some are looking with confusion. You tell everyone we are not practicing, we are about to pray and then minister before God and his people... You pray and feel such warfare and discard, this feeling, you haven't experienced before.

You arrive to the stage; Jezzie is dancing all over the place including doing her own moves. Her chaos has caused the other dancer s to be off trying to figure out what's going on. The other dancers are so off right now trying to figure out what is going on. The unity of the dancers is missing; they are divided because a Jezebel spirit has been allowed to come on board. A Jezebel spirit comes to wreak havoc, bring discard and confusion into the ministry. Leaders, be aware of those you allow on your team; you must operate with the spirit of discernment.

Jezebel Spirit is proud and arrogant, one that goes against delegated authority, refuse to submit. Jezebel means unmarried; meaning operates in the flesh and is not connected. We are married; we are connected to the spirit of God and are humble. As we flow in the spirit we produce the fruits of the spirit and we are submissive, kind and obedient. Jezebels carry many signs, arrogance, deception, hidden agendas, pride, jealousy, rebellion, mind control, anger, envy competition, a spirit of control to name a few. Leaders if you encounter or run into the Jezebel spirit, immediately deal with this spirit, it comes to tear down and destroy ministries and homes, marriages, relationships, do not be intimidated by this spirit. Dance leader go directly to your Pastor and address this issue. Do not let these spirits destroy or tear up your ministry. Definitely keep the person before God to be delivered and to shine a light on them that they are operating with a Jezebel spirit.

Exodus 34:14

14 For thou shalt worship no other god: for the LORD, whose name is Jealous, is a jealous God:

Chapter 9

He wants it All

Our God is a jealous God......... Exodus 34:14

Worshipers God didn't make it a secret but he said it and he said it loud and clear, He also meant what He said. He is a jealous God. Praise dancers, if God says He is jealous and says don't place other Gods before Him, why would some of you worshipers go to the club Thursday, Friday and Saturday night twisting, shaking and dropping using your vessel in the club dancing with satan and all his imps and pimps. On Sunday morning, you want to dance before God and His people because you practiced on Monday, Tuesday, and Wednesday, and you have a leading part and you know you can dance and you know you can get the crowd moving.

Again, God is a jealous God, why would anyone be bold enough to bring contaminated and filthy worship to a Holy God, coming before Him and His people with no shame or remorse. Oh, because the church wasn't at the club, your pastor wasn't at the club nor were the saints there, so what, you had a good time and because you twisted so hard with the devil and you received some phone numbers. Well I come to tell you that yes, your church family wasn't there, but Jesus was in the building. The Almighty one, The Holy and Righteous God, all seeing and all-knowing God was there and that type of performance does not please Him. Why would you go before God and his people and give him a perverted, unholy worship when he won't receive it because it stinks before His nostrils.

Matter of fact it breaks God heart that we would be more worried about performing our gift than giving Daddy God a sweet and Holy worship in dance, or song and or in the preaching of the Word. No one is exempt. Dancers, I hope I have your attention. Did you know many churches despise praise dancing and wish the leaders and Pastors would do away with it? Problem is many praise dancers have no conviction and are unruly, stuck on their gifts and their self-image instead of being a True Worshiper, equipped in Holy Armor, A consecrated worshiper. Even when taught about it, they refuse to live clean but want to dance before our Holy King. It's a sad thing, and many don't see anything wrong with it. One reason may be that many leaderships cover it up. Because they are gifted and anointed, or they are not anointed but entertain so well people are moved by their emotions and began to give all their money to have the dancer and the leader use that dance to raise money for the ministry.

We do have anointed dancers that are set apart for God, that fast and pray, and live upright before God ushering in His presence with the ministry of dance. I know that all dancers are not wild and dishonoring God their gifts and themselves. God has a great team of true worshipers.

So, what happens? The result is we see unconsecrated worshipers who have not given their all to God move with lustful and provocative movements, dancers trying to be sexy, or performing for attention so people can see them and their curves News flash!! Praise dancing is not your time to shine and or hoping you get a phone number from the pew or pulpit, that's not it. Jesus is a Holy God, what is done for Him, must be done in decency and in order. We are to follow in his footsteps.

Think about this, Jesus in the biblical days out preaching and teaching, sweating in the blazing sun, there was no air conditioner or building for protection from the elements. How would it have looked if Jesus had taken off his shirt to preach? No, not good. With that being said what you wear and how you wear it to minister is very important; make sure it's appropriate for the audience and pleasing to God.

He wants it all; yes, He does every drop of our flesh. To do better, we must know better, and that is the purpose of my book to shine light on dark areas, areas that most won't talk about or get mad about. I believe as you are reading your eyes will be more open and your spirit will be alert to what God is saying and what He wants from his worshipers. Dancer, as I keep looking and thinking over what the Lord have shown me through the years, I must not forget our men. I have witnessed on several occasions when a praise dancer is up ministering, but the moves are so sexual and provocative, that the men are feeling uncomfortable and you see wives mad and basically threaten their husband about watching these praise dancers. Our men are being deprived and feeling guilty, because they want to enjoy what everyone else is enjoying. Dancers, please take all of this into prayer and into consideration. Our men are being robbed, because of what is designed to be pure and holy is tainted with lust. Dancers, let's give it all to God and get completely delivered.

God wants it all! But to give Him all of us, we must want to give our whole self to Him and want all of Him too. That day when the struggling dancer makes a decision to be pure and Holy before God and his people the enemy will scatter and run screaming. The devil knows when true worshipers take the stage, true deliverance and healing will manifest; the lame shall walk, and the angry shall have peace and love, sickness must flee. The word of God said greater works shall we do. To do the greater works, we have to die to our flesh the greater. Dancer, God wants all of you, your brokenness, disappointments, hurt, pain, rejection, pride, arrogance, low self-esteem, rebellion, lust, He wants it all so that He can pour all of himself in you, and through your worship his power shall manifest. Dancers, you will dance the dances of the Lord continually as you give Him all of you and He will lead and guide us to our next song, assignment, event, etc.

Prayer: Lord Father I come now repenting of all knowing and unknowing sins. Lord, I want to give You all of me. Father wash me, cleanse me, purify me, search me, deliver me. Oh God, I want to be more like You and less like me and I want more of You. Thank you, God, for purging me and hearing my heart's cry. In Jesus Name.

Amen!

2 Corinthians 10:13

13 But we will not boast of things without our measure, but according to the measure of the rule which God hath distributed to us, a measure to reach even unto you.

Chapter 10

"Dance Away of Escape" ....2 Corinthians 10:13

Dance is my way of escape from everything. My worship, my dance is my safe place, my love place, my place of acceptance, my place of reassurance, my place where chains are broken and strong holds are pulled down. When I enter God's presence, seeking to be in His presence, I receive deliverance. Dance has been my way of escape in many situations, naturally and spiritually. In the natural, when I was in the world, I would be lost in my dancing; dancing was my purpose and mission. To go to the club and get on the dance floor felt like me and the music and dance floor became one. Well we did. It was deeper than how it made me feel on the dance floor, but we became one and the very words of the songs began to talk to me. I responded to what they were saying. I know that last line you just read may have you scratching your head. Don't worry I will explain.

First, we are spirit, then flesh. When we were born, we didn't know that the spirit was operating in the inside of us. Before we are saved and receive Jesus, we are connected to everything good and bad and in between in the spirit. Most of us have experienced music and dance from family gatherings, parties. We learn that the sound of music makes us move, clap our hands, nod our heads, move our feet, and or shake our hips. Many of us grow into adults and keep pursing that feeling too.

Not knowing that all along the Lord deposited worship on the inside of us. If we are not aware or our purpose and shown how to grow in that purpose and develop it God's way, it will be used for the wrong purpose. We could end up dancing with the wrong partner. Many worship dancers have a need to dance and what happens is the enemy gets a glimpse of your future and the impact that you will have in ministry. The devil's purpose is to get us off focus and keep us blind regarding our purpose. He sets many traps along the way because his main reason is to ensure we don't fulfill God's. If you don't know who you are and who lives in you, that wonderful plan that God has for you many never be manifested in your life. For the weapons of our warfare are not carnal but mighty through God to the pulling down of strong holds.

One of the enemy's greatest tactics is to send manifold trials into our lives; these trials are to keep us focused on one problem after another; thusly, we miss our destiny. As a praise dancer, dance is your weapon. As we know, operating in our gift will not only get us delivered, but we go to the pits of hell through our worship to bring out others.

I was speaking earlier about how I became one with the club music. Those songs talked about having a good time, drinking, smoking; others talked about making love, cheating in the next room, and I can't live without you; the words of the songs and the spirit that comes from them talked to me. There are even songs that encourage murder, drug use, and greed. The ears are the gates to our soul and when we listen to this music over and over again, it gets into our spirit and encourages us to act accordingly. This opens the doors to spirits good and bad.

I am sharing this to shine light on the knowledgeable of sprits as they relate to music. In the world we live in, many church leaders are struggling with sin, sex, lost identity. Music is powerful and it speaks to us in a way nothing else can. So just as I was speaking earlier about the secular music sending a negative message, we can listen to a positive message in a worship song, but if the spirit is tainted or contaminated we then open ourselves up to the spirit that the singer or psalmist is struggling with.

We must get delivered first before we minister before God and His people. I had to go through a deliverance process as well; I kept falling into fornication. And the crazy thing about it was it would happen soon after ministering either later that day or within a few days. I would find my whole body awaken and very much alert, very sensitive. After falling a few times in the sheets, I went to my Pastor. Dance N2 ur Deliverance. I told her what was going on. I was embarrassed but I wanted help, I didn't want to fall into sin anymore, especially after being with God and in His presence. It made me feel so low and unworthy. I cried out to God.

My Pastor explained something to me that I had never heard. She said anytime we enter in an intimate place with God He awakens every part of us. All parts of our body are awakened, first because He created our whole body. She explained that many ministers have fallen weak right after ministering, because they didn't have a covering or someone to explain to them what was going on with their body. That was a time to be in God's presence not falling into somebody arms or bed.

Dancers, we must dance the dance of God, but to know that we must read and studied the word as well as fasting and praying. God gave us the gift of dance it is a powerful deliverance ministry. We have the honor and privilege to dance the dance of deliverance at funerals, weddings, church, retreats, and many other events. Many people get delivered through the dance because of the passion and love we have for God and God's people. Dance takes people to another level, sometime the Word may not reach them, but God gave us the powerful opportunity to reach them through dance.

We must know the power of dance and music. To dance to your deliverance, we must know the spirit of God and who you are in the dance ministry. As teacher, Prophet, Evangelist, Apostle, what is your role in the kingdom as a worshiper dancer/ demon slayer? An Atmosphere changer! Dance is such a powerful tool God used Prophetess Miriam as she sang and danced leading other women in the dance with their tambourines while dancing and singing a song of victory for Moses unto God. (Exodus 15:1;20).

Dance as a way of Escape. Initially, God gave each and every one of us a gift, a unique gift. The gift He gave us is 3-fold; first it's for the Lord to give back to him. Second, it's for the body of believers and unbelievers. Third, it's for us as God uses our gifts to heal and deliver others; through our obedience and faith we receive deliverance as well.

Dancer, I want you to know that you are not just a praise dancer; you are a mighty warrior, tearing up and demolishing satin's kingdom. Look at how God has positioned us, we have gone from the church to funerals, weddings, Mayor and council meetings to minister through dance. Many people want it for the entertainment aspect of it but God has made a way of escape for others to get delivered and receive salvation through the dancers.

I was one of those dancers that didn't want to minister at a funeral or a musical. At funerals, we minister to a lot of hurting, and unsaved people. That's why God wouldn't send me. They needed to escape right into the heavily realm so deliverance will take place, opening their hearts for salvation and healing.

Dancer/ worshiper, you are somebody and deliverance follows you anytime you surrender and dance the dance of the Lord. You will dance into your deliverance and send others into their deliverance. Dance as a way of escape at family gatherings, family reunions, graduations, picnics, concerts, God is opening these doors for us to minister to bring deliverance to God's people and our love ones. Dance a way of escape, some dancers don't like to talk or minister verbally but God says your dance is your voice, your weapon to help set the captives free. You are a minister, preaching the word through motion, mime, hip-hop; however, the Lord gives it to you, use your weapon of deliverance.

How can you boldly walk in the anointing to bring deliverance to yourself and God's people while being pleasing to God?

1. You must be saved and sold out for Christ, Holy and acceptable… (Psalm 19:14)

2. You should be willing to let go of your will and thoughts and fully walk in Gods will (Luke 22:42)

3. You should go through a spiritual cleanse, and deliverance for yourself, through the word of God(Luke4:18)

4. Pray these scriptures over yourself (KJV)Psalm 51:1-19, Luke 22:42, Jeremiah 31:13

5. You must bind and cast down the spirit of fear and unworthiness. Know that You Are God's true worshiper (2 Timothy 1:7)

6. You must know you can do all things through Christ who strengthens you. (Philippians 4:13)

7. Lastly you must know that the thoughts and plans God has for you are good and not evil

8. (KJV) Jeremiah 29:11

9. (greater works)

Prayer: Lord Father, I just want to thank You for calling and choosing me to be Your worshiper and giving me away of escape through the dance, arts, music. Lord father, I thank You for deliverance and cleansing and understanding of who You say I am. Lord Father I agree with you.

I love you Lord. Amen

Exodus 28:41

41 And thou shalt put them upon Aaron thy brother, and his sons with him; and shalt anoint them, and consecrate them, and sanctify them, that they may minister unto me in the priest's office.

Chapter 11

Consecration & Consummation Exodus 28:41(KJV)

Consecrated – 2a: to make or declare sacred, especially to devote irrevocably to the worship of God by a solemn ceremony, set apart, dedicated, hallow (transitive verb Merriam dictionary)

Exodus 28:41 (KJV)

To be consecrated means to be set apart for the masters uses. I love being used by God, how about you? You know there was a time that I didn't know what it meant to consecrate myself. All I knew was God saved me and called me to dance for him.

I did just that, while living a life of fornication. I didn't intentionally want to be there, but I had just come through a divorce and was hurting; I met someone and fell into fornication while still going to church and praise dancing.

When I tell you, it was the most horrible feeling ever to fall into sin and then be asked to minister through dance the next day or so.; it was horrible. A strong conviction fell over me because I wanted to be holy and pure before God, but my flesh wanted to be satisfied. One day I talked to my pastor, not many can go to their pastors without being stoned. I bless God for my Pastor, Apostle Neddie Moore, I could be transparent, and real with her because I wanted help and deliverance.

She began to talk to me about having a fasted and consecrated life. She would give me assignments, to read the word of God, specific scriptures, also she would instruct me too fast. I was given instructions on what not to listen to on the radio and what not to watch on television; and no talking on the phone after hours with the opposite sex.

The purpose of the scriptures was to kill my flesh with the word of God and to strengthen my spirit, through fasting we kill our flesh, for we know that the spirit is willing and the flesh is weak, by praying the prayer of deliverance we build up our spiritual man. As I followed this plan, God began to deliver me. Also, God was able to deliver me because I wanted to be delivered.

A consecrated life is a pure life. You are set apart, in this world but not acting like the world. We don't talk like the world and we don't do or go were the world goes. As a consecrated worshiper, we are not just holy on Sunday and wearing clothes that cover us at church, but on Friday and Saturday night we expose ourselves. A consecrated life is a life style that never goes out of style; it's lived every day.

Dancers we should consecrate ourselves on a regular basis. Fast, pray, anoint ourselves, and study the word of God for strength to withstand the temptations that are coming our way. Dancers are to be a responsible vessel living a life of consecration; you have to have a partner who will make you accountable to the truth. A God-fearing bible talking and living saint who will tell you the whole truth.

Dancers we want sincerity, we don't want to give our God a perverted, fornicating, filthy dance, but we want God to be glorified and pleased waiting for us to come in His presence to worship Him. Dancers I don't care if you're on a dance team and the leader never commits to fasting and praying, never reads a scripture; then you be the shining light, but be it in love.

Living a consecrated life not only keeps us from the sheets, but it kills our pride, arrogance, and competitive nature, so we are able to walk humbly before God and man.

Dancers even those secrets sins such as masturbation, maybe you're not sleeping with a man, but you participate in masturbation. I pray that you will get delivered from that spirit as well. I struggled with that spirit; we must confess it to God and ask him for deliverance. Dancers, we are spirit and flesh therefore, these sins and struggles we don't want to put in the atmosphere through our on struggle.

Worshipers, that is why it is so important to stay prayed up with regular fasting to stay pure and holy before our Almighty God. And we feel good about ourselves and our works in the kingdom.

Prayer: Lord, I pray that I am the vessel of honor used for Your purpose. Lord Jesus, I ask You to give me a heart of consecration and repentance, I want to be Holy, I want to be right before you Lord. Father, forgive me for coming into Your presence any kind of way. Today Father, I confess my sins before You and ask You to wash me and make me whole, for I decree and declare I am Your consecrated worshiper. Amen

Consummation- Joining together, to become one,

Coming together as one. This is God's heart cry for you and me, to be one with Him. When we look at the word consummation, one of the definitions describes the wedding night, the joining of husband and wife in the marriage bed, the two becoming one. When intimacy between the two comes together, the man penetrates the woman. Let's go deeper, in this process the man steps inside of the women and the two become one, this is a powerful example of intimacy that is twofold.

This act of consummation is what our heavenly Father wants to have with us His worshipers, His dancers. You may be asking how I can truly become one with God. We must be intimate with Him and the first thing we must do is have a plan and a special place just as we would prepare for our husband or wife.

Set the atmosphere with praise and worship, set a time to meet with our Father, anoint that place where we meet with our Father. To have an intimate relationship we need all these tools in operation. Worship with a pure heart and give our whole self to him; tell Him how much we love Him and need Him. Now that you have His attention, God will come and step inside of you and you and Him shall become one. Now you are able to hear and carry out the plans and instructions that He has for you in your life and ministry.

When this takes place, we have to give up all rights and let Him lead, let Jesus wrap His arms around you and speak to you. It's easy to receive when you have set an atmosphere to be loved on and want to be intimate. In this place God can down load vision, dances, songs, and places to go and minister. Dancers, you want to keep a life of consecration and consummation with the Lord; it keeps open the communication line between the both of you. It keeps you in the plan and will of God.

As we are in this place, it keeps the flesh dead and our spirit alive, so that we know that it was and is God that we live, move and have our being. It's not in our gifts and talents and all the years of dance training we have had, and it's not in the great platforms that we have had the privilege to dance/minister on, but it is in a consecrated /consummated life. Not that we soar, but that God will release healing and deliverance in the atmosphere. This place of submission will change the mind of God. Hear and obey so that you can experience God in your dance/ worship on another level, realm and dimension.

Ezekiel 44:19

19 And when they go forth into the utter court, even into the utter court to the people, they shall put off their garments wherein they ministered, and lay them in the holy chambers, and they shall put on other garments; and they shall not sanctify the people with their garments.

Chapter 12

Cover Yourself .... Ezekiel 44:19

Cover yourself in his righteousness before we can cover ourselves with Holy garments. We must prepare our minds and spirits to come into the presence of God and to go before the alter of worship before His people who are looking to us to come with holy worship in order that they may receive a greater determination to live and go on a little bit further.

Let's spin toward our Dance Leaders. Dance Leaders are called to lead they will teach and lead. Leaders lead by example. What we see, we do, we imitate. Dance leaders we must check our leading skills and make sure that they are lined up with the word of God and not our fleshly, arrogant ways.

Dance leaders we should teach about Holy covering. I've noticed that as new dancers come into our dance ministries, many are put in leadership positions and have no former leadership training. They go by what they think or what they have seen on YouTube. And what the Pastor is saying, who most of the time do not have knowledge of the dance ministry either.

Dance leaders, we want to teach and stress how important it is to be covered in righteousness as well as the right attire. We have talked about righteousness a little in this chapter but the chapter before definitely broke down how to get in a righteous place with God.

Let's look at attire: For every dancer no matter the age, shape or size

#1 Leotard that fits, and padded bra not a sports bra unless padded and it shouldn't' crisscross at the neck.

You do not want your straps showing. Leotards are good to keep everything from moving and it covers the stomach and arms if long sleeves. When we wear our leotards either wear an overlay or fabric wrap.

Don't just wear a leotard. No one should see the size of your breast whether small, medium, or large.

Dancers we want to take all attention off our body parts as much as possible. We want to be a witness not a hindrance for someone's deliverance because the whole time we are dancing they are looking at our breast.

Bra- we all should wear a padded bra. When we get cold the headlights pop out. No one should have to watch your nipples as you mister, and it affect the witness and the power of how God wants to move. And most men are very uncomfortable, that 's unfair to them, and it could hinder them from receiving from this ministry, because they are trying to stay in the spirit, but your nipples are speaking louder than the music. Dancers don't hinder your witness, pad yourself.

 Bra- we want a good bra with good support to make sure your breast is not bouncing up and down. and or the bra is too small and you are sticking out on sides or top. Let's use wisdom and good judgment when ministering.

Dancers if you are ministering in white use black underwear and bra, remember no red hot, pink polka dots, red, green etc. (Either plain or the one with cover underneath).

#2 Leggings/Palazzo Pants-. All dancers should wear leggings and palazzo pants, in this 20th century there are a lot of dancers doing kicks, rolls leaps and jumps. And the leggings don't cover completely. Dancers, we want as less of our body flesh to be shown as possible.

Leggings- when you kick or spin your thighs and butt are more likely to be shown. As we know everyone isn't saved and some are saved but not delivered. Dancers use leggings and palazzo pants so you will be covered...

#3 Skirt/dress Dancers again this is not a time to be sexy. Our skirts should fit so it doesn't fall off around the waist, but they should not be form fitting or short. We are Holy worshiper's dancers for the Lord, not for America has Talent. The same thing applies for the dresses. None should be skin tight or low cut. Overlay and wrap if your dress is fitted around the breast /chest area.

The items I just listed are the basic items you should have for your dance ministry and for your dancers.

When choosing dance garments, pray about where to purchase them. If custom made pray for that person, contact them and order.

Dancers, when we receive our garments pray and anoint your garments. Pray over everything that you will wear to minister in including under clothes and foot wear. Dancers if you don't possess a Bible or anointing oil invest in these. We must cover ourselves in the word and the anointing oil.

Our Bible, the word is a covering and we must cover ourselves in the word of God. We will be dressed in holiness, purity, humility and humbleness. Clothed in his righteousness.

We should cover ourselves with good character and integrity. Dancers, we must have integrity in all things. Remember, we don't take any or all engagements; only those that exemplify Christ and His Spirit. Don't accept engagements just because you are invited to minister. Don't clothe yourself in entertainment but be clothed in the spirit of ministry. Don't be covered in arrogance or pride but be clothed in humility and have a servant's heart, we should be clothed in the garment, heart of a worshiper.

Cover yourself in the beauty of holiness and truth; clothe yourselves in prayer. Once you cover yourself in these garments, then we can go and put on our sacred garments.

Biblical Colors (KJV) scripture & meaning

White- Purity, Holiness, Righteousness, Triumph, Surrender, Angels, Bride, Priestly Garments, Light, Saints, Peace, Victory, Glory

Scriptures: Isa.1:18, Dan. 7:9, Dan. 12:10, Mt. 17:2, Jn.20:12; Rev. 3:4-5, 6:2, 7:9 Ecc. 4:8

Yellow- Counsel of God, light, joy celebration glory revealed.

Scriptures: Isa. 51:11, Isa. 61:3, Heb. 1:9

Silver- Redemption, Word of God, Freedom, strength, atonement, divinity, righteousness, strengthened faith

Scriptures: Ex.30:13-16, Ps.12:6, Zec.11:12-13, Mt.26:14-15 Proverbs 2:1-5

Red- (Scarlet, Crimson) Atonement, sacrifice, consuming fire, war, courage, murder, blood of Jesus, covenant of grace, cleansing justification, sin, death, love, life, redemption, person of Jesus, the cross.

Scripture- Gen.9:4, Isa. 1:18, Lev. 14:52, Lev.17:11 Rev. 1:5 6:4 12:3, Joshua 2:18

Gold- Deity, wealth, kingliness, refining fire, the Godhead, glory, purification, Divinity, majesty, righteousness, divine light, mercy

Scriptures: Ex. 37:6, Rev.1:13014 @Chr.4:20-22, 9:17, 20 Rev.3:18

Green- Flourishing, new life freshness, new beginning, vigor, prosperity, praise, eternal life, Gods Holy seed, harvest, sowing and reaping

Scriptures- Ps.58, 92:14, 37:35

Blue- Heavenly, Prophetic, Holy Spirit, grace, authority, seated with the Lord in heavenly places.

Scriptures: Ex.24:10, Num.15:38, Eze.1:26

Brown- man, earth Gen. 1:10

Black- Death to self, hiding place sin shadow of His wings, Affliction, Death, mourning, Humiliation, famine, distress, suffering, darkness, evil, curses

Scriptures: Lam. 4:8, Mal. 3:14, Jer. 8:21, 14; 2 Ps.17:8, 18:11, 23:4, 97:2 Eph. 5:11

Bronze- brass, copper- Judgement, Fires of testing

Scriptures- Exodus 27:1-3, Exodus 30:17-21

Blue- Scarlet Jesus as the God- man

Burgundy/wine – New wine, the cup of the new covenant, blessings, rejoicing, blood of Jesus, Bride of Christ, surrender, and the fellowship of Christ suffering

Scriptures- 1 Corinthians 11:25

Purple- Royalty, Kingship, majesty, wealth, kingliness, power, mediator, penitence, the name of God, kingdom authority, dominion, son ship, the promise of God, inheritance

Scriptures- Ex.28:8, Esther 8:15, Jud.26, Dan.5:7 Jn 19:2, Mk 15:1, 7 &17-18

Pink (rose) Messiah, glory, rose of Sharon, right relationships, church, fathers, love, joy, compassion, heart of flesh, passion for Jesus, the Bridegrooms heart

Scriptures; Roman 3:25

Orange- Praise warfare, passion, power, fire, harvest season, fruitfulness, joy

1 Chr. 23; 13, Ps.113:3

Fuchsia- joy, right relationships, compassion, heart of flesh, passion for Jesus, the Bride grooms heart

Multi-color- jubilee, all nations-tribes, Apostolic, Favor of the Lord, (gold, blue, purple, scarlet, white)

Scriptures: Lev. 15:9-10

1 Corinthians 6-17

But whoever is united with the Lord is one with him in spirit.

Chapter 13

Dance with Me

Spirit and Flesh Dance Together as One

1Corinthians 6-17

I believe we all want to experience the presence of God and His Presence. Even greater, we want to dance with Him. In order to have this oneness with God, we must have an attitude of worship. We have to prepare the atmosphere to meet with Jesus. Most major events of healing, deliverance, and change comes through worship, instruments; worship gets God 's attention and changes his mind.

We want to be with God, and in order to be one with Him and dance with Him, here are steps we should take.

1. Fix our minds on Jesus, not our situations, job, family, etc.

2. Create a special place to meet with our Father.

3. Set the atmosphere with song, worship, frankincense myrrh and oils.

4. Prepare our heart for repentance, ask God to create in us a clean heart and renew the right spirit in us.

5. Invite Him in, matter of fact; give Him free range to have His way with you.

To dance with the Lord, we must invite in His presence and once He is there, we want to yield our heart and spirit to Him. We want to move in sync with him; therefore, we must be sensitive when He begins to speak. Prophecy falls great when we are in deep worship and have yielded to God and just let go and let God have his way. It's during these times, we come vulnerable to the spirit of God and now He can twirl us with his finger or flip us up and down in midair, because we have relinquished our mind, body to the Lord and now He is having his way with us.

During this time, we receive the dance of the Lord and a dance with the Lord. Yes, I love it. There's no other place I'd rather be than dancing with my Father, my creator, the one who put the gift of worship in me.

Dancers don't be afraid to allow the Holy Spirit to take over and lead the dance. I remember the first time God took me in the spirit, and I begin to spin like a whirlwind and the first few times when I came out of it, I fell on the floor, fearful that I was going to hit something or hurt myself. And, the fear of the people in the room connected to my fear and made the fear real loud in my ears.

I kept dancing and eventually entered another realm with God, because I loved the way I felt dancing with Him and Him dancing with me and through me. I finally got comfortable with dancing with my Father. I then could identify who I was and what the purpose of the spins was. Through prayer and seeking wise council as well as being in a prophetic atmosphere, I found out that God was using my spirit to do warfare in the spirit realm, tearing up the fowl ground, softening heartened hearts and regulating troubled minds. The Lord was dancing in me and through me His spirit in me brought about deliverance to the people when I ministered. Then the Lord revealed to me that I was a Prophetic dancer as well.

Through learning how to tap in the spirit and prepare my atmosphere for my heavenly Father, other gifts manifested. As of today, I minister heavily in healing, deliverance and prophetic dance, warring in the spirit. As believers, we want to be carriers of God's presence, we want Him to dwell on the inside of us. We want to feel Him, hear Him and move with Him. When we allow the Holy Spirit to abide in us and we in Him the impossible will take place. Dancers, it's not in our dance technique, although dance technique is good, but it's in us being carriers of God's presence and keeping our hearts pruned and open to Him. This will allow us to dance the dance of the Lord, sing the song of the Lord, pray the prayer of the Lord, and preach His word.

As we do these things we will experience the power of God like never before; change and transformation will happen before our very eyes. The word of God gives us an example in 2King 3:13-15. When Elijah needed to make a wise decision about the battle about to take place, he went to hear from God. But first he asked for the minstrel and as the anointed minstrel began to play, prophecy began to fall. Dancers, be sold out for God so that He can stir you with more gifts and ignite you with greater fire, power and anointing. Dancers go and allow the Spirit of the living God to intertwine with you, turn you, flip you, speak to you and set divine order in your spirit. You are now equipped to go deeper in the spirit of worship. I hope that you have received revelation, answered questions and peace of whom you are and who your Daddy is. Now Go and Dance with your Father!

Lord Father, I come now in the Name of Jesus giving myself away; I desire to be one with You and You with me. I surrender my body, spirit, gifts to You. Lord, I give You every hindrance that will hinder me and You to become one. My spirit is leaping because I will dance with my Father. **Amen**

Hebrew / Greeks words DANCE

(Strong's Concordance)

1. CHIYL-(2342) –Or chiyl {kneel}; a primitive root; properly, to twist or whirl (in a circular or spiral manner), i.e. (specifically) to dance, to writhe in pain (especially of parturition) or fear; figuratively, to wait, to pervert -- bear, (make to) bring forth, (make to) calve, dance, drive away, fall grievously (with pain), fear, form, great, grieve, (be) grievous, hope, look, make, be in pain, be much (sore) pained, rest, shake, shapen, (be) sorrow(-ful), stay, tarry, travail (with pain), tremble, trust, wait carefully (patiently), be wounded. Judges 21:21

2. MACHOWL (4234) - a (round) dance Psalm 30:11, Jeremiah 31:4

3. MECHOWLAH (4246) a dance / company of dancers Judges 11:34, Exodus 15:20

4. DALAG (1801) to leap or spring. Song of Solomon 2:8, Isaiah 35:6

5. CHAGAG (2287) to move in a circle/ march in a sacred procession/ celebrate a festival/ dance.

Psalm 42:4, Zechariah 14: 18

6. KARAR (3769) to dance or whirl 2Samuel 6:14

7. RAQAD (7540) to stamp/ spring about/dance/jump/leap/skip 1Chronicales 15:29, Ecclesiastes 3:4

8. PAZAZ (6339) to spring or leap 2Samuel 6:16

9. PACACH- (6452) to hop/skip over/ to dance 1 Kings 18:26

10. GIYL/GUWL (1523) to spin around under the influence of emotion (usually rejoice) 1 Chronicles 16:31, Psalm 9:14

11. ALATS (5970) to jump for joy/ be joyful/rejoice/ triumph Proverbs 28:12

Greek Words for Dance & Worship

(Strong's Concordance)

Dance

ORCHEOMAI (3738) to dance Matthew 11:17

CHOROS (5525) a round dance Luke 15:25

AGALLIAO (21) jump for joy/ rejoice greatly Matthew 5:12 and Revelation 19:7

SKIRTAO (4640) (4640) jump for joy Luke 1:41 and Luke 6:23

Words for Worship

PROSKUNEO (4352) to worship, to kiss (like a dog licking its master's hand) to prostrate oneself in homage John 4:23, Revelation 7:11

LATREUO (3000) to serve, minister, worship Philippians 3:3, Luke 2:37

Dance in the Bible

There are references to show that dance was part of Israel's culture. It still is today!

Jephthah's daughter- Judges11:34

Ladies dancing in the vineyard- Judges 21:21-23

Children playing games- Matthew 11:17

The return of the prodigal son- Luke 15:25

Celebrating victory 1 Samuel 18:6-7

Dance is associated with joy and contrasted with Mourning- Lamentations 5:15, Psalms 30:11, Ecclesiastes 3:4

There is to be dancing (and joy) when Israel is restored- Jeremiah 31:4&13

Miriam led dancing, singing and praise-Exodus 15:20-21

David danced before the Ark of the Lord-2 Samuel 6:14-23, 1 Chronicles 15 and 16

We are to praise God with dancing- Psalms 150:4, Psalms 149:3

Other references in the Bible to lively worship included dance. Hebrew words that have meanings related to physical movement were translated into English as "rejoice"

The Hebrew word for tambourine is TOPH (Strong's 8596)

The tambourine has been used since ancient times.

Laban wanted to send Jacob and his family away with music- Genesis 3:27

Job speaks about people who played music and tambourines, but did not want to know God- Job 21:12

The Hebrew word for playing a tambourine is TAPHAPH (Strong's)

The tambourine was used in warfare and to celebrate victory.

The Lord defeating his enemies to the sound of the tambourine- Isaiah 30:32

Miriam led the women in praising God for His deliverance from the Egyptians Exodus 15:20

Celebrating David's victory over the Philistines- 1 Samuel 18:6

Jephthah's daughter meeting him after his victory- Judges 11:34

The tambourine was used in praise and worship

Prophets using the tambourine and other instruments

1 Samuel 10:5

2 Samuel 10:5

1 Chronicles 12:8

Psalms 68:25

Psalms 81:2

The tambourine is associated with dance

Psalms 149:3

Psalms 150:4

Jeremiah 31:4

See also some of the previous references

Exodus 15:20

Judges 11:34

1 Samuel 18:6

The Hebrew words used in the Old Testament for flags and banners are:

DEGEL (Strong's 1713/1714) means to be conspicuous

NACE (Strong's 5251) means a signal

OWTH (Strong's 226) means a signal

We are pointing people to Jesus in our praise and worship.

Advice to leaders

Leaders we must first have a heart of worship. A heart that seeks the face of God and his will only. Open to his voice and what he Desires to do through the ministry and each person.

1. As leaders you must always walk in love. (1 Corin.13:2) Without love it will not be unified and will not exemplify who Christ is he is Love.
2. As leaders, you should have a short bible teaching and express reading the word, fasting and prayer. Leaders explain to your team that you can't minister in the spirit expecting God to move when your vessel is empty or fleshly. A life style of the word, prayer and fasting is a MUST!!!
3. You need to be creative in your choreography, be enlarged in your creativity. Don't stay in a box, God is spontaneous and loud and cheerful not dead and boring. Let God release fresh movement that speaks to the dancers and the people.
4. As leaders go abroad be enlarged also bring in professionals, leaders don't be intimidated by bringing in someone to take your team to another level. Leaders use those on your team who have been trained or are more skilled in some areas. One body, but many members. They should all work together.
5. As leaders, you need to learn how to be aggressive when it comes to (handling business) and shutting down discard and or chaos. To many times leaders just don't want to hurt people feelings. Sometimes leaders don't want to address the situation because they themselves can't handle confrontation. But if you are a true leader, and you don't handle a situation that is clearly out of line, then it will spread like wild fire in your team and ministry and will bring division and all kinds of breaches. Leaders we must be aggressive, shut it down, sit them down, speak to them and bring correction. Keep it moving, still all done in love.

6. Stick to Practice Schedule day and Time. Leaders don't allow free and down time to be an enemy in your practices and rehearsal. Weed out sitting around and talking. Short breaks for water and restroom are ok. You have a job to do in rehearsal and that is to make sure everyone is on the same page, moving together as one. You cannot effectively do that if there is free time.
7. As leaders have a plan/ vison and stick to your agenda to keep a steady teaching flow. Have an outline/agenda to follow. Always lead the vision and agenda that you have; always have a goal in mind. Know where God is leading the ministry and the message. Leaders, you're being prepared and ready will keep the team fired up and excited to see what God is saying and showing you. It will make it easier to jump and stay on board.
8. Leaders you should have expectations of your team. Explain to them your vision, passion, and purpose. Let them know their role in helping this unfold. Outline their responsibility as a team member on paper. Then hold them accountable to their commitment.
9. As leaders, you need to make yourselves available to your team members they should feel comfortable sharing with you their concerns. They have to feel that they can trust opening up to you with real situations, issues, concern. They need to know that you care about their hurts and needs. They may not like your answer, but at least they feel they can come and talk to you.
10. Leaders, (if you are leading a dance ministry inside the church) I feel it is needful to have an outline of your job description from your Pastor(s) what does your Pastor envision for the dance ministry. What does he want you to accomplish in the dance ministry? By getting a clear understanding from your leadership, it will help you cultivate the dance ministry to work hand in hand with the vision of the church.

Team Players (dancers)

As team members, take responsibility of your spiritual life and obligations unto God and the ministry. It is your responsibility to grow in the word and in your ministry.

You have a responsibility to passionately seek the face of God and humble yourself to his call for your life. Knowing that He will keep you and lead you to the right leaders to pour into your life and give you a place of expression.

1. As a team member, your roll is to push and support the vision and the leader.
2. Uphold your commitment to the team. You have a responsibility to be present and carry out your assignment and if you are not able to make a rehearsal call and get with team members to go over dance choreography.
3. You need to be a person of your word. If you commit to 1 or 2 practices a week, then be a person of your word and integrity, follow through responsibly.
4. It is your responsibility as a team member to be on time to practices and be at every practice.
5. Pray for your leadership and ask God to strengthen them, give them continued wisdom and discernment the focus to carry out the vision and creativity.
6. Always go to your leader and tell her about anything you're feeling or anything you might have an issue with. Never go to another team member. If you take your issue to another team member, then you are being used by the enemy to sow seeds of discord in the ministry. And never go over your team leaders head by going to the Pastor or overseer of your department. Go to your team leader first. That is the order of God.

7. Pay attention to detail of choreography and do not wait till practice to practice. You need to take time between rehearsals and go over the choreography yourself and make sure you know it. This will allow the leader to move forward in teaching and not have to continually go back and review something they have already taught.

Worshiper!

God has called you to be His worshiper, a dancer for Him. You were called to dance and eradicate the plots and plans of the enemy. Dancing the dance of deliverance.

"Spirit and Flesh Dancing together as One" was written so that you can tap into a realm of worship that you have never experienced, by equipping you, giving you truth and strategies to overcome the temptations that worshipers struggle and fight with. You will know that you were handpicked to be the Glory carrier of God's presence. Atmosphere changer! You have danced before the King, but now you will learn how to dance with the King.

Spirit and Flesh Dancing Together as One.

Dancer of Eradication

Made in the USA
San Bernardino, CA
24 February 2018